Joseph-Gray
we enjoyed
having you
visit us
at the
Calgary Comedy
Mom & Grandma

Thanks for
coming to
visit with
Mom. I'm
so glad you
had so much
fun. We
love you
dearly.

With love
and always
today and
Aunt Donna
& Karen - Uncle
& Ken - Michael, Luke

xoxo

A Merry-Mouse Book
of Favorite Poems

A Merry-Mouse Book of Favorite Poems

PRISCILLA HILLMAN

Doubleday & Company, Inc.
Garden City, New York

MERRY-
MOUSE
BOOK™

Dedicated to the memory of my father

Grateful acknowledgment is made to the following for permission to reprint their copyrighted material.

"Little" reprinted by permission of G. P. Putnam's Sons from Everything & Anything by Dorothy Aldis. Copyright 1925–27; renewed © 1953–55 by Dorothy Aldis.

"The Mitten Song" by Marie Louise Allen. Copyright 1946 by The Association for Childhood Education International. Reprinted by permission of the author and the Association.

"Mud" by Polly Chase Boyden from Child Life Magazine. Copyright © 1930, 1958 by Rand McNally & Company. Reprinted by permission of Barbara Boyden Jordan.

"The Cupboard" from Collected Poems by Walter de la Mare. Reprinted by permission of the Literary Trustees of Walter de la Mare and The Society of Authors as their representatives.

"Mice" by Rose Fyleman from Fifty-one New Nursery Rhymes. Copyright 1931, 1932 by Doubleday & Company, Inc. Reprinted by permission of Doubleday & Company, Inc., and The Society of Authors.

"The End" from Now We Are Six by A. A. Milne. Copyright 1927 by E. P. Dutton & Co., Inc.; renewal © 1955 by A. A. Milne. Reprinted by permission of the publisher, E. P. Dutton & Co., Inc., and the Canadian publisher, McClelland and Stewart Limited, Toronto, and of the British publisher, Methuen Children's Books Ltd.

"The House of the Mouse" from Another Here and Now Story by Lucy Sprague Mitchell. Copyright 1937 by E. P. Dutton & Co., Inc., renewal © 1965 by Lucy Sprague Mitchell. Reprinted by permission of the publisher, E. P. Dutton & Co., Inc.

"Animal Crackers" (first three stanzas) in Chimneysmoke by Christopher Morley (J. B. Lippincott Company). Copyright 1921, renewed 1949 by Christopher Morley. Reprinted by permission of Harper & Row, Publishers, Inc.

"Three Guests" by Jessica Nelson North, reprinted by permission of the author.

"After the Party" by William Wise. Copyright © 1956 by William Wise. Reprinted by permission of Curtis Brown Ltd.

Library of Congress Cataloging in Publication Data

Hillman, Priscilla.
    A merry-mouse book of favorite poems.

    SUMMARY: A collection of poems, including old favorites and new ones.
    1. Children's poetry, American. 2. Children's poetry, English. [1. American poetry—Collections. 2. English poetry—Collections] I. Title.
PS586.H5   811'.008'09282
ISBN: 0-385-17104-8 Trade
ISBN: 0-385-17105-6 Prebound
Library of Congress Catalog Card Number 80-2551
All Rights Reserved
Printed in the United States of America

THE SWING

by Robert Louis Stevenson

How do you like to go up in a swing,
　Up in the air so blue?
Oh, I do think it the pleasantest thing
　Ever a child can do!

Up in the air and over the wall,
　Till I can see so wide,
Rivers and trees and cattle and all
　Over the countryside—

Till I look down on the garden green,
　Down on the roof so brown—
Up in the air I go flying again,
　Up in the air and down!

ANIMAL CRACKERS

by Christopher Morley

Animal crackers, and cocoa to drink,
That is the finest of suppers, I think;
When I'm grown up and can have what I please
I think I shall always insist upon these.

What do you choose when you're offered a treat?
When Mother says, "What would you like best to eat?"
Is it waffles and syrup, or cinnamon toast?
It's cocoa and animals that I love the most!

The kitchen's the cosiest place that I know:
The kettle is singing, the stove is aglow,
And there in the twilight, how jolly to see
The cocoa and animals waiting for me.

MICE

by Rose Fyleman

I think mice
Are rather nice.

Their tails are long,
Their faces small,
They haven't any
Chins at all.
Their ears are pink,
Their teeth are white,
They run about
The house at night.
They nibble things
They shouldn't touch
And no one seems
To like them much.

But I think mice
Are nice.

DOWN RASPBERRY LANE
by Priscilla Hillman

As we hurried with our basket
down Raspberry Lane,
our clothes were splashed with water
from a recent rain.

Ahead we saw the raspberries
drying in the sun,
and putting down our baskets
we picked them one by one.

We stained our mouths and fingers
as we nibbled on this treat,
and soon we filled our baskets
with all that we could eat.

TO NANA'S
by Priscilla Hillman

I'm waiting to go to Nana's house
as I sit here in my best.
My Mom won't let me out to play
for fear I'll soil my dress.

I love to go to Nana's house;
she is so nice to me,
and makes me tasty carrot cake
and lets me sip her tea.

I picked some pretty flowers
to take along with me,
and I know that she will love them,
because they are from me.

AFTER THE PARTY

by William Wise

Jonathan Blake
Ate too much cake,
He isn't himself today;
He's tucked up in bed
With a feverish head,
And he doesn't much care to play.

Jonathan Blake
Ate too much cake
And three kinds of ice cream too—
From latest reports
He's quite out of sorts,
And I'm sure the reports are true.

I'm sorry to state
That he also ate
Six pickles, a pie, and a pear;
In fact I confess
It's a reasonable guess
He ate practically everything there.

Yes, Jonathan Blake
Ate too much cake,
So he's not at his best today;
But there's no need to sorrow—
If you come back tomorrow,
I'm sure he'll be out to play.

A KITE

Author Unknown

I often sit and wish that I
Could be a kite up in the sky
And ride upon the breeze and go
Whichever way I chanced to go.

THE DAFFODIL

by Priscilla Hillman

I opened up my window wide,
and saw a daffodil
nodding gracefully in the breeze
under my windowsill.

It lifted up its yellow head
and seemed to hum at me,
and then I saw within its cup
a golden bumblebee.

THE HOUSE OF THE MOUSE

by Lucy Sprague Mitchell

The house of the mouse
is a wee little house,
a green little house in the grass,
which big clumsy folk
may hunt and may poke
and still never see as they pass
the sweet little, neat little,
wee little, green little,
cuddle-down hide-away
house in the grass.

A WISE OLD OWL

Author Unknown

A wise old owl sat in an oak.
The more he saw the less he spoke.
The less he spoke the more he heard.
Why can't we all be like that wise old bird?

SUNDAY STROLL

by Priscilla Hillman

We often take a Sunday stroll
on a golden sunny day,
and eat delicious ice cream cones
as we amble on our way.

Our Mama lets us buy balloons
of yellow, pink, and green,
and the flowers by the cobbled path
are the loveliest we have seen.

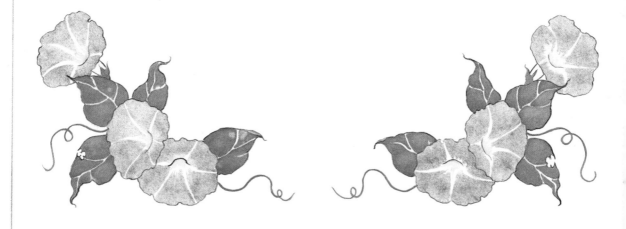

LITTLE

by Dorothy Aldis

I am the sister of him
   And he is my brother.
He is too little for us
   To talk to each other.

So every morning I show him
   My doll and my book;
But every morning he still is
   Too little to look.

THE DANDELION

by Mrs. E. J. H. Goodfellow

There was a pretty dandelion,
  With lovely, fluffy hair,
That glistened in the sunshine
  And in the summer air.

But, oh! this pretty dandelion
  Soon grew quite old and gray;
And, sad to tell, her charming hair
  Blew many miles away.

CLEANING DAY

by Priscilla Hillman

Squirrel is busy on house-cleaning day,
with a brush, some soap, and a pail.
She washes the windows, the kitchen, and floor
and sweeps out the dust with her tail.

THE CUPBOARD

by Walter de la Mare

I know a little cupboard,
With a teeny, tiny key,
And there's a jar of Lollypops
For me, me, me.

It has a little shelf, my dear,
As dark as dark can be,
And there's a dish of Banbury Cakes
For me, me, me.

I have a small fat grandmamma,
With a very slippery knee,
And she's the Keeper of the Cupboard,
With the key, key, key.

And when I'm very good, my dear,
As good as good can be,
There's Banbury Cakes, and Lollypops
For me, me, me.

THE SQUIRREL

Author Unknown

Whisky, frisky,
Hippity hop,
Up he goes
To the tree top!

Whirly, twirly,
Round and round,
Down he scampers
To the ground.

Furly, curly
What a tail!
Tall as a feather
Broad as a sail!

Where's his supper?
In the shell,
Snappity, crackity,
Out it fell.

THE MITTEN SONG

by Marie Louise Allen

"Thumbs in the thumb-place,
Fingers all together!"
This is the song
We sing in mitten-weather.
When it is cold,
It doesn't matter whether
Mittens are wool,
Or made of finest leather.
This is the song
We sing in mitten-weather:
"Thumbs in the thumb-place,
Fingers all together!"

THE LITTLE BUSY BEE

by Isaac Watts

How doth the little busy bee
Improve each shining hour
And gather honey all the day
From every opening flower!

THREE GUESTS

by Jessica Nelson North

I had a little tea-party,
This afternoon at three;
   'Twas very small,
   Three guests in all,
Just I, myself, and me.

Myself ate up the sandwiches,
While I drank up the tea,
   'Twas also I
   Who ate the pie
And passed the cake to me.

THE LETTER
by Priscilla Hillman

*I wrote to you my sweetest friend,
for I longed to have a chat.
I wrote all kinds of lovely things,
about just this and that.*

*I licked a little four-cent stamp
and put it on my letter;
then telling Mom I was going out
I buttoned up my sweater.*

*As I ambled down the windy lane
among the leaves of gold,
I snuggled deeply in my sweater
for it was getting cold.*

*Among the twisting vines and leaves
the wooden mailbox hid.
I put my little letter in
and closed the wooden lid.*

*I hurried back the way I'd come,
under the cloudy sky,
and the wind tugged my skirt about
as it went rushing by.*

SAILING

by Priscilla Hillman

Ducky goes sailing on clothes washing day
in a basket, with sheets for a sail.
He dreams he is sailing far out to sea,
fighting the storm and the gale.

THE END
by A. A. Milne

When I was One,
I had just begun.

When I was Two,
I was nearly new.

When I was Three,
I was hardly Me.

When I was Four,
I was not much more.

When I was Five,
I was just alive.

But now I am Six, I'm as clever as clever.
So I think I'll be six now for ever and ever.

MUD

by Polly Chase Boyden

Mud is very nice to feel
    All squishy-squash between the toes!
I'd rather wade in wiggly mud
    Than smell a yellow rose.

Nobody else but the rosebush knows
How nice mud feels
    Between the toes.

THE RAIN

by Robert Louis Stevenson

The rain is raining all around.
It falls on field and tree.
It falls on the umbrellas here
And on the ships at sea.

THE CREATION
by Cecil Frances Alexander

All things bright and beautiful,
All creatures great and small,
All things wise and wonderful,
The Lord God made them all.